A Young Black Man

By

Lorenzo C. Spencer

A Young Black Man

© Copyright 2015, 2023 All rights reserved worldwide by Lorenzo C. Spencer.

Spencer Truth Publishing
ISBN-13: 9780692529225
Paperback (2nd version)

All rights reserved. No part of this publication may be reproduced, stored in a retrieval system, transmitted in any form or by means-electronic, mechanical photocopy, recording, or any other- except for brief quotations in print reviews, without the prior permission of the publisher and author.

Warning: I used the word nigger to convey a message in some of my poems and thoughts. I used * in place of some letters to spell out words. In certain instances, my grammar style might not be proper grammar, but I used certain words and phrases to create my writing tone.

Disclaimer

A Young Black Man is a non-fictional book, but I used fictional characters and situations in my parables to convey a message. The material contained in this book is purely informational and informative but not intended as professional advice. The author is not responsible for use/misuse of this information and takes no responsibility for the outcomes resulting from the use of this material.

Acknowledgements

I would like to thank my Lord and Savior Jesus Christ. I would like to thank my wife and daughter. I would like to thank every member of my family and friends who supported me or prayed for me. I would like to thank all of my brothers, uncles, cousins, nephews, grandfather, and father. Even though I might not be able to spend much time as I would like with you, I still love you.

I would like to thank the leaders that came before me. The ones who gave their lives, so that I am able to write, read, and express my thoughts on paper. I would like to especially thank all of the young Black men who know how to rise above day-to-day issues with a positive solution.

I would like to thank everybody who spoke some truth in my life. I would like to thank my editor Shaletha MC Davis and everyone who participated in the A Young Black Man Video. I would like to thank my teachers, pastors, and every young Black man who have great insight.

I would like to thank everyone who read this book and all of the parents, grandparents, etc… who lost a loved one to the struggle.

Table of Contents

Insight Behind My Writings 7

Youthful Thinking 9

On The Young Black Man 9

Young Black Man 10

The Plan Of A Young Black Man 12

A Positive Young Black Man 15

How To Be A Young Black Man 18

Under The Circumstances, It Is Hard Being A Young Black Man 20

Don't Stereotype The Whole Generation Of Young Black Men 23

Help The Young Black Man 27

Don't Stereotype A Person Because Of Fear 31

Wisdom Thoughts 35

Youthful Thinking 38

On Racism and Prejudice 38

Racism, Prejudice, And Envy Are Our Enemies 39

Stop Racism Before It Is Too Late 43

From Their Birth It Is A Clean Wipe Slate 45

Positive Men Take A Stand 47

Wisdom Thoughts 49

Youthful Thinking 52

On Getting an Education	52
Get An Education	53
The Key Is A Better Education	56
Wisdom Thoughts	58
Youthful Thinking	61
On Trusting Someone Else	61
So Trust Yea Not In A Friend	62
Enemy In The House	64
In Order For A Man To Understand	67
Wisdom Thoughts	68
Youthful Thinking	70
On Life, the Ghetto, and Other Things	70
Life Is Worth Living	71
It Is So Easy To Do Negative Things	73
Perished By His Lying Tongue	76
Treasure Of Gold In The Sky	78
Stuck In The Ghetto	80
Wisdom Thoughts	82
Reflections on Today's Issues	84
Justice Or Else	85
Black Lives Matter	86

Who Do You Protect?	*88*
The Code Of Silence	*90*
Can't Think Straight	*91*
Weigh Every Word For Truth	*92*
The Women Movement	*93*
Who Are You Following?	*94*
Random Thoughts	*96*
Could There Be A Leader To Come Up Out Of Memphis?	*98*
Wisdom Thoughts	*99*
Thoughts About Family	*101*
He Is A Father To His Child	*102*
I Don't Have Time	*105*
Father Where Are You?	*107*
Wisdom Thoughts	*108*
Thoughts About GOD	*110*
So Many Questions	*111*
Wisdom Thoughts	*112*

Insight Behind My Writings

There is hope for the young Black men. There was hope for me. I was raised in two projects in Memphis Tennessee. I experienced what it is like growing up with the odds stacked against you. God chose to use me. The Holy Spirit spoke to me one day and He said, "Teach my people." I begin to write and compile this book on a young Black man from some of my older writings.

I was inspired to write at a young age. I was in high school penning my thoughts as I talked to God not really fitting in. I didn't really understand then, but now I do. I always cared passionate about the issues of the day. I guess you can say that I was conscious-minded.

I remember writing in solitude and embracing nature as I told my story on paper. I also remember writing about being a young Black man, love, life, God, and understanding.

I was seventeen at the time and I wrote several notebooks of poetry which I am now sharing some of my thoughts with the world. I titled each series of poems *Youthful Thinking* because they were created from my youthful perspective.

I am also sharing with the world *Wisdom Thoughts.* Wisdom Thoughts are my current views on today's issues and wisdom that I gained from God on the past different subjects and issues.

At the end of each series of *Youthful Thinking*, I will leave you with my *Wisdom Thoughts.*

What good would a book on being a young Black man be, if I don't speak on the issues of today? I will leave you with new poems and thoughts which the series will be titled *Reflections on Today's Issues that Faces Black People.*

After God commissioned me to write this book, I asked Him a Question.

I asked God, "Is there hope for the young Black men?" He said, "You have to speak positively over their life instead of negatively over their life." There are many people who think that there is no hope for the young Black men. They negatively speak out loud and to them it is a fact. I believe what God said, "There is hope for the young Black men." We have to speak positively even when we don't see it yet.

I believe there is hope for the young Black men. I believe that one day that we shall rise and be all that God called us to be.

Youthful Thinking

On The Young Black Man

Young Black Man

Why call me a nigger?
Like I am some low-down dirty figure
Am I a main too?
Do I have the same thang you have too?
Why are you taking me through all of this trouble?
Is it true that underneath our skin that we are the same color?
Do you see me or my skin tone?
If you just see my color
You are dead wrong
For my skin might not be light
But my IQ is very bright
I might not be sexy and fine
But I am a unique individual with a powerful mind
You may call me nobody
But to God, I am somebody
I really don't care what you think
Because my destiny is up to me
Yes, because I am a young Black man
I got one strike against me
I am going to prove

To you, you, and you
That I can make it in society
Look into my deep eyes
Then you will see my great Black pride
I am not racist or prejudice
I believe all races should assimilate
I just ask for a chance
To be a young Black man
Before you stereotype me
Look deep inside of my thoughts
And you will really get to know me
Understand my pain and misery
So don't lock me out in the dark
I hope you realize
It is hard to be a young Black man in society
Because life is still a challenge
And I will face that challenge day to day
My bible is my sword
As I press along the way
Traveling through the dark and dreary lands
With knowledge and wisdom, I shall stand
For I am a young Black man

The Plan Of A Young Black Man

Why do other people refer to me as a low-down person?
Who has no destiny?
Someone who don't care about society
Why do people love to judge me?
Always saying all young Black men sell drugs
Thinking that all young Black men are thugs
I know that it is true that a lot of Black men are in jail
It is also true that it is a logical reason behind the stories that people tell
But all young Black men don't sell drugs
And all young Black men are not thugs
I have dreams too, as well as a plan
It is obvious that I am a young Black man
When you look into my eyes
You shouldn't be surprised
When society put me down
I will continue to walk with a stride while closing my ears to their lies
Keeping my foot planted on a solid ground

For a solid foundation
I have found
If you have not heard
These are the words
Of a young Black man
Telling every person in his community
Rather he is a White man or a Black man
To stand in unity
I am not a racist but a man
For this is the dream of a young Black man
I just want people to understand
That every young Black man
Isn't a negative man
I guess a rotten apple destroys the bunch
But I won't be crunched
Just because of my fellowman
For I am a young Black man
For this is the dream of a young Black man
That every color of men
Stand in the covering of unity
For the future of the world
Is up to you and me

Now is the time to take that grandstand
And walk and talk
As we together hold hands
So that the entire world can see
Every color of men
In this great land
Standing for Justice
For this is the plan of a young Black man
As we walk and talk with each other
With an open dialect
There is more to discover
I will learn to understand my brother
Then and only then we will be able to learn from one another

A Positive Young Black Man

I am a young Black man
It is bad enough
That the other men misjudge me
It hurts my heart to know
That the older Black men think we won't be able to stand
Because of how they view the younger Black men
They think that we can't achieve
Our goals in life
The older Black men really don't believe
That we will be able to stand
Some criticize us, and give our generation no help
Now who is really deceived?
With Jesus Christ helping me to understand
I know that I can achieve
There isn't any doubt in my mind
I shall rise up
It might take a little time
All I ask of my fellow man
And especially of the older Black men
Don't stereotype me because I am a young Black man

All I ask is for a fighting chance
To stand and be a young Black man
And to my fellow brother man
Because you finished college with a degree
I know that I graduated from the streets
Don't look down at me
Are you better than me?
It still doesn't give you the right to judge me
I am a person with feelings
Someone who is willing
To better himself
Before I self-destruct myself
You are a man like me
Open up your eyes and see
A young Black man who wants to be
The absolute best that he could possibly be
Like the grain of sands
There are plenty of positive young Black men
So give me a fighting chance
So that I can give proof to everyone
That I am truly a young Black man
With positive plans

I am here to stay, and I will stand
And be counted as a positive young Black man
So other Black men who found good jobs
Help me out, don't look down upon me
You of all people should know that it is hard
For I am struggling in my community
To be a good role model
For other young Black men in society
I hope every young Black man will follow me
I am focused on God, family, and community
All I ask for is a fighting chance
To be a young Black man
So don't judge me
By my credit score, my color, or my creed
But let my character speak for me
Please use wisdom and try to understand
Sometimes things aren't what it looks like
I am a positive young Black man

How To Be A Young Black Man

Under the circumstances
It is hard being a young Black man
I live in the ghetto
Surrounded by crack and dope
Sometimes, I can't cope
The only thing that I have is my hope
So I ran and ran
From the problems of life
But they still keep coming back again and again
I tried to fight
For each day is a struggle for my life
I tried to find a job
I know it don't justify the fact that I rob
But I see life as money, money, money
My life is so depressed
I don't even look for the day that is sunny
For every day of my life has been gloomy
My father never talked to me
He never showed me
How to be a man

But now I am looking to Jesus for a better plan
Can you really heal me?
Do you really care about me?
My father never loved me
Jesus, I am in search of my identity
I am without my earthly father's helping hands
So I am asking for your help Jesus
Help me be a great young Black man
Take away my gloomy days
Let no money rule over me
Help me to enjoy life
Give me hope in you
Enable me to stand
Show me how to be a positive young Black man

Under The Circumstances, It Is Hard Being A Young Black Man

Some people just don't understand
Under the circumstances
It is hard being a young Black man
I only have a mother
I never knew my father
She took care of me and my brother
She taught us with her limited amount of knowledge
My mother never graduated from college
By her not being a man
She lacked some details on how to teach us
On how to be strong young Black men

She worked two jobs at night
I knew then that my future wasn't very bright
Struggling by herself to pay the bills
Many nights, we went without lights
But she took care of her little men

Some people don't understand
That under the circumstances
It is hard being a young Black man

I was persistent
One day, I wanted to be able to pay the rent
That is why every day I went for my education

People told me
That I won't be anything
But I followed my dreams
I faced difficult situations
And a lot of humiliation
Like going to school
With a hole in my shoes
Walking to school in the cold
Standing up bold
I didn't always have name brand clothes
The children called me names
Many times I have been ashamed
But nothing could stop me from getting my education
And learning more new information

But I am still blessed
Because God continue to help me stand
For I am a young Black man
Most people don't understand

That under the circumstances
It is hard being a young Black man

But I shall persevere
I shall persevere through the storm
I shall persevere through the struggles
Even though struggling seems to be my norm
Each day I am faced with a new set of circumstances
But each time I overcome
I am becoming a better young Black man

Don't Stereotype The Whole Generation Of Young Black Men

Just because one young Black man is a negative person
There is another young Black man who is a positive person
So don't stereotype the whole generation
Of young Black men
Give every young Black man an equal chance
To be a young Black man
For a young Black man
Is a suffering man
Who tries to understand
Why people sometimes say,
"He is less than a man"
A young Black man is also a spiritual man

You should consider
Just because my fellow man robs
I am not a criminal
I have a good job

Each day of the week I do work
On Sunday I do go to church
My fellow man
Might can't make a good decision

And don't believe in God
But I got my religion
And I do make mistakes because of some bad decisions
But I am not a negative person
Just because he is a bad person
So don't stereotype the whole generation
Of young Black men
Give all young Black men an equal chance
To be a young Black man
I am sorry that my fellow man
Killed your mother
True enough he was my brother
But everyone isn't like the other
He is a murderer that kills
I am a doctor who is trying to heal

So when you see me
And you just see that I am Black
And you immediately think that every young Black man doesn't know how to act
You are dead wrong

You are only viewing my youth and my skin tone
For I am a citizen just like you
I am intelligent just like you
I am not an ignorant man
Anything you can do
I can do it as well as you can
For I am a young Black man
My brother might be a negative person
But I am a positive individual
So don't stereotype the whole generation
Of young Black men
Give all young Black men an equal chance
To be a young Black man

Every young Black man
Isn't an ignorant man

Isn't an unintelligent man
Isn't a crazy man
Isn't an illiterate man
So don't believe the hype
Think before you start to stereotype

Help The Young Black Man

My great grandparents were brought to this land
Chained up by their hands
Millions of people like the grain of sands
In small beat-up ships
Brought to this newfound land
Shipped across the ocean and sea
With shackles and chains on their feet
No food they had to eat
But in Africa they had plenty of meat
Some wicked White men captured the children, women, and men
And took them to an unfamiliar land
The open ocean took many to their graves
The rest were purchased as slaves

Many years later they were freed
But the white southern hatred hung them on trees
The Civil Rights Leaders came along
They marched to a different tone
Some used violence

Others used Civil Disobedience
But still the Black man
Though he was oppressed
He still stands
Searching for a better plan
In search of equality
All of the brothers stood in harmony
They fought for education
And Voter Rights of Registration
It was a struggle for the Black man
But still they did stand
The Civil Rights Movement
Built up the young Black men confidence
The Black people won another victory
For everyone wanted harmony
And they were together in unity

Now in this day and time
We, young Black men have a job to do
There is a large amount of young Black men who are locked up for crimes

In some instances overcrowding the jail cells
Because we as a people somewhere failed

Our strong communities and society have also failed
True, there are a percentage of young Black men locked up behind bars
Maybe for stealing cars
Maybe for selling dope
We positive young Black men
Need to start restoring hope
To the other young Black men
Let us stop all this inner hate
And let us help one another before it is too late

We can't get sidetracked by doing petty crimes
We must start using our minds
Every Black mother and father should take a stand
And participate in help raising up positive young Black men
For we are an endangered race
So young Black men take a stand

Push past your circumstances
Society, lend us a helping hand
Pitch in however and whenever you can
We will appreciate it
Try to eliminate some of the struggles of young Black men

For the Black men who have already made it
Don't forget about helping other Black men
Who are trapped by the system
Please give them some positive insight and wisdom
Please extend your hands
And help out another young Black man
Our motto should be if *I stand then I will help another young Black man who wants to stand*

Don't Stereotype A Person Because Of Fear

The world is filled with tears
People are walking around
They are all in fear
Some people seem to be getting scared by the year with their reality
Some older people thoughts are unclear
They think that every youngster
Is a robber or gangster
Because of fear

When some young Black men walk in the store
The manager watches him
They act like they dropped something on the floor
The store clerk calls a code U
The whole work crew
Report to the front of the store
The security guards begin to trail you out of the door
What for?
Because you are a young Black man

So they think that you are going to steal something out of the store

I have learned through the years
The people of the world are in much fear
Fear of the younger generation
They think the youngsters
Make every situation into a negative situation

When we speak out
Out of desperation and frustration, we may shout
Because every store we step inside
The security guard or store owner eyes
Are glued to our side
Because we are Black and young
They think that we are going to steal
You can see them clutching their guns
Sometimes they make us feel like criminals
Stereotyping every youngster who wears fashionable clothes
Leaving our stories untold

When people watch me like a criminal
It makes me want to explode
And let off steam

With thoughts of knocking down a wooden beam

People who stereotype me
Most of the time, they know nothing about me
Other than I am a young teenager
With a cellphone
That is hanging with other teenagers

Somehow, we don't get credit for working in the community
Or being a positive figure in society
Some people just love to bring the worst out of people lately
It isn't our fault that you shed a tear
Or the world is in fear
What I am trying to say while making it clear
I know life isn't fair sometimes
It is getting dangerous every year
Violence and more violence are steadily on the rise
If you watch the news, then more violent stories are all you will hear
Who won't be in fear?
But don't stereotype a young Black man's clothes
Before you judge him

Get to know his inner soul
And I know being a security guard is hard

But every young Black man who comes in the store
Isn't coming to rob
So give them some space a part
Quit watching every young Black man on the premise of him being young and black
If you do, then subconsciously it might make them want to take or attack

Why?
Because if they are not criminals
It makes them feel like criminals
The negative thoughts that you might instill in their minds
Might make them want to commit the crime
I know life sometimes make some people fearful
True, it is getting dangerous every year
But don't stereotype a person because of fear

Wisdom Thoughts

I was not spared of the thoughts and reality of being a young Black man. What is super crazy is that I get stereotyped by my own people today.

I guess I got a criminal look and walk. Wait one minute, what is a criminal look and walk? Last time I checked criminals come in all varieties. Some criminals are White, Black, Asian, or Latino etc.... with clean-cut and rough faces.

I have been discriminated against in my Sunday's best. I have to laugh because my work clothes have often raised suspicious behavior to the store clerk or owner who has checked me out at stores.

When this happens on a constant basis, you tend to feel some type of way. Let us just say, "It isn't positive." If you top off this negativity with the stress of everyday life, things can easily get out of hand. It can easily go from 0 to a 100 quickly.

You might have to often remind yourself that you are too blessed for mess or stress. Stress is not just a young Black man's problem. It is a society problem. Some women are dealing with no loving and no caring baby daddies. Some young men are dealing with unthankful and ungrateful baby mommies. Let us get back to the subject at hand. Too much stress, along with the extra things a young Black man goes through can cause you to act some type of way.

On the other hand, you can be one of those people who act like things don't bother you or you can address the issues. It all starts with you admitting that there is an issue.

I have learned that people will be people, but you can choose to react positively to each situation. This will help control the flow of things. Your decisions affect you. It is true that the way some people feel toward you might affect you slightly. Let's be honest to ourselves, greatly! But you have the power to overcome and pull through any negative obstacles that stand in your way.

There will be times when people really think that you are a nigger. Other times, people will stereotype you for no reason at all. You have to keep your head up high and fight through each difficult circumstance.

Sometimes, I do feel out of place when I am stereotyped for no reason at all, or I am faced with difficult circumstances. I just don't let other peoples' feelings define me. What defines me is what I think of myself. What defines you should be what you think of yourself.

Do you think enough of yourself to not portray or act out on how negative people perceive that you should act, or do you have enough courage to act better? It's your life. Choose Wisely!

You can have two types of attitudes. One type of attitude is I am. The other type of attitude is I am what they said I can be. Now which type of attitude do you have? A young Black man attitude must be I am.

When a person or persons say negative things about you, you should say, "I am a positive young Black man." "I do have a plan." In other words, your speech should reflect you in a shining new light.

You must speak positivity into your life and gradually act the part. You must always remember that action speaks louder than words, but a new you begin with a renewed mind.

Youthful Thinking

On Racism and Prejudice

Racism, Prejudice, And Envy Are Our Enemies

We are not ignorance to the fact
Self-confidence we should not lack
Respect of one creed
Is a common thought we must all heed
A person with common sense
Know prejudice and racism is wrong
We must all repent
If we practice this evil wrong
Teaching one is inferior over the other
God is our Holy Father
How can a man have supremacy over his brother?
Calling his brother man
Less than a real man
White supremacy is wrong
Black supremacy is wrong
Anyone race supremacy is wrong
But human supremacy is right
All colors of people black and white

Fighting for what is right
Truth, justice, and freedom

Racism and prejudice we shall overcome
With the bond of brotherhood
But still there will be some
Who will never act right
Who will continue to fight
For the wrong things in life
Like Black domination of the world
Or White domination of the world
Or any one race domination of the world
So we must be strong
And hold on
To what we believe in
For this world is full of sin
But God's people shall truly win
As we come together in harmony
As we fight for equality
God is our Father
That is the words I utter
By Jesus Christ, we are all brothers

Why say that you want to dominate your brother?
The seed of your mother
You have no love for him
Or no compassion for him
But you want to rip his head off with the claw
You wicked men like Esau
You have wronged your brother by creating unmoral laws
You call yourself a Christian
A friend to God to the end
But Christ gave his life
For all people
It doesn't matter your color or creed
As long as you believe
For brotherhood is livelihood
A brother is trustworthy
He has no envy or jealousy
Racism and prejudice are his enemies
People of all creed and colors
Are truly sisters and brothers
Seeds of our Father

When we come to this enlightenment
We will stick together
And fight our enemy forever
Racism, Prejudice, and envy
Then no dark cloud will any longer linger over our hearts forever

Stop Racism Before It Is Too Late

Is every man treated equal?
We as the people
Must stop the shackles of racism
With the bond of love
And guidance from above
We must thrive
And our great nation shall rise
For justice and peace
Our spiritual man will never cease
To fight for what is right
Until he knocks out racism

A soldier may fight in the street
He might get beat
And he will start to retreat
He will come back again
Each time until he does win
Because suffering makes him rise again
Let us not wait for our great country to fall
Let us tell our children about the negativity of racism

When they are small
Because a child doesn't know more than what a parent teaches them to know
Their parents are the ones who should instruct them daily as they grow
So don't teach a child how to hate
The other different race
Before it is too late
Teach your child how to embrace the other race
For goodness' sake
Let us stop racism before it is too late
Because a face is just a face
Color doesn't matter
God loves us all
That is what really matter
Not if a person is large or small
Because our mindset determines our nation faith
With racism this generation shall fall
If we stop racism, it shall stand tall

From Their Birth It Is A Clean Wipe Slate

A child doesn't know how to hate
A child doesn't know how to be prejudice
From their birth it is a clean wipe slate
A child doesn't know how to be racist
A child doesn't know how to use criticism
From their birth it is a clean wipe slate
They learn by their parent's mistakes
Or what their parents teach them about the subject
If their parents teach them about respect
In most cases, they will have respect for people
Treating everybody equal
If you teach hate
Your child will learn how to hate
Children don't learn hate when they are born
From their birth it is a clean wipe slate
So parents should teach
As the preacher should preach
The holy truth is not a lie
The moment your child start asking why

Teach them to be respectable
Teach them to be responsible
Teach them to believe in God
Teach them so they can grow strong
Teach them that we are all children of God
And in God's eyes
All men whether his color, financial status, nationality, or social status are all the same
We all can be saved in Jesus' name
By all means don't teach hate
Don't teach prejudice or racism
But teach them faith
Cause from their birth it is a clean wipe slate

Positive Men Take A Stand

With God as your guide
You shall rise
With a positive attitude
You shall rise
The limit is the sky
All you have to do is try
To do the best you can
Be your own best man
Create a powerful master plan
Learn to understand
How to become a positive man
A positive man helps others become better
So if I fail, it is because I am trying to help someone else get to the next level
If we fail
Let us fail
Trying to make things better
Today the young Black men are facing a storm
For no ship sails alone in extreme weather
Without any fuel trying to discover new shelter

The bulletin reads extreme weather
You have been warned
All men on deck
It is time to take heed
All positive role models take a stand
Because there is a need
Help our young Black men
Stand up
Stand up for peace
Stand up for equality
Stand up for liberty
Stand up for unity
Stand up for justice
Stand up for human rights
This is a public service announcement for all positive men
To help a weak man who doesn't understand
How to be a strong and positive man

Wisdom Thoughts

It is funny how so many people want to pretend that racism and prejudice doesn't exist in this day in time. Some people might say, "That the young Black man is just crying, boohooing, and whining." Some people might say, "A Black man has been elected twice to the president's office, so surely racism is a thing of the past."

The response from me would be laughter. Ha-ha-ha, the joke is on you. Any person with a little bit of wisdom can see what the evil powers that be is trying to do. Racism and prejudice are on a much greater scale. The gap is steadily being opened wider and wider with all of the propaganda in the media.

It is time to open up your eyes if you are still sleeping. Once you wake up to this known fact, it is time to react. There is nothing like unknowingly becoming a part of racism and prejudice. We are at a point when things are coming full speed. If you don't make a conscious decision to be on the side of truth and justice, you could be forced to take a racist stand on some of today's issues.

Some people might say, "How does this affect a young Black man?" When you or I are manipulated to agree with any injustice just because of race, it is a discredit to us (A young Black man).

The name of the game is manipulation and the evil powers that be have been doing it to us for years. Some of our leaders have taken part in covering up the truth, so that we can participate in racism and prejudice. The key to stopping it is not adding to it.

We must keep an open mind and not just carry every torch or cause just because a person looks like us. We must weigh the person or persons according to the deeds for the issues at hand when they call for our support on injustice.

It is up to us to take stands that won't set us back. We must know why we are doing what we are doing? How will it affect our community when we do engage positively?

As we, young Black men take the brute of racism and prejudice on our shoulder, we have to be the bigger man and not dish it back out. We have a choice. Let us not be manipulated in choosing the wrong choice.

It is easily said than done. I know that under the most difficult circumstances we can beat the odd and let impartial justice be our calling card.

I too feel the pile of bricks weighing down on my shoulders when someone discriminates against me deliberately. Even today, I feel the pressure of being a young Black man. But I know what they don't know, they can't break me. I can choose to react negatively or positively.

I know that our fight can be won. We don't have to keep singing *We Shall Overcome.* We can overcome without striking a physical blow. Someone said, "It is all about who you know." I know Jesus!

Youthful Thinking

On Getting an Education

Get An Education

A long time ago our people marched
They marched with brotherhood
And with a lot of love in their hearts
Many people are being robbed
Because many people fought for Civil Rights
Brave people gave their lives
Some people don't appreciate the rights
That we gained in the Civil Rights Movement
A long time ago
Our forefathers before
Couldn't be educated because of their pigmentation
Now we have a chance for a free education
Because the Civil Rights Leaders built us a foundation
Because our fathers were persistent
They gained a lot of accomplishments
At first, they faced humiliation
There was a lot of lamentation
Among our wildest imagination
But they pressed for perfection

The prejudiced people showed no affection
Our forefathers stuck together with cooperation
And overcame the situation
The Civil Rights Leaders earned the rights for us to go to school and learn
So they kept America standing firm
They fought for their children's education
Now some children don't want to learn any new information
That the educators teach in school
Some children rather pop pills and smoke blunts because they think it is cool
It hurts my heart
When a youngster drops out of school
Since we gained the rights
For a free education
Some people have forgotten about the struggles for Civil Rights
Dropping out of school have no self-justification

How many Black people gave their lives?
Our forefathers put up a good fight
They wanted a great education
Now since we gained that right
Dropouts give off a misrepresentation
To the whole Civil Rights cause
So wait a minute and pause
Please remember the Blacks and Whites who gave their lives in time past
Just so you could be able to read
Educate yourself because knowledge is vast
As your knowledge begin to multiply
In your heart, you will know
That the Civil Rights Leaders just didn't die
For no reason at all
But they did die for a worthy cause
So that you could walk down the school halls
So that you could sit in the classroom learning vast amounts of new information
While you get an even higher and higher education

The Key Is A Better Education

One key to overcome the woes of life
Is a better education
It could better your situation
An education enhances your chances
As a productive young Black man in society
It opens the door for better advances
For the world is full of qualified competition
If you choose to drop out of school
You really don't know what you are missing
A chance to be the absolute best that you can be
You are missing a chance to present your parents with your degree
Do you know that a High School Diploma is a steppingstone?
College is in a class of its own
So don't stop now when you get your High School Diploma
You have to move on
Press forward
Don't go backward

Never say die
Grab your pie
In the sky
You are reaching new levels
As you continue to fly
Please take full advantage of a higher education while it is free
If you fail to take advantage of it
Blame yourself and stop blaming society
So if you don't like your situation
Remember that one key to overcoming the problems of a young Black man
Is a better education

Wisdom Thoughts

An education is a great tool to have in your bag when you are facing life challenges as a young Black man. It gives the people who intentionally discriminate one less weapon to use against you.

You should believe me. It will come up if you are trying to move up in a company or on a job. There will be some requirements that everyone who is not privileged must follow.

Mostly every time when a company or job wants to discriminate, they do it in stealth mode. If they see that you lack a higher education, then they make sure that the job posting requires it. My answer to this is you must know the game and play it well.

If your reason for not wanting to finish high school or to attend college is because what the educational system teaches, then you might want to reconsider. You have to know how to be a critic who weighs his or her options. It is alright to have an opinion but will that opinion stop you from earning more money in the future.

I will use a person who doesn't want to go to college because he thinks that the educational system brainwashes people for an example. John never researched the facts, but he believes it. Why? Because John's friend told him that he saw that going to college brainwashes people online. You must use your common sense.

John must ask himself a few questions. Did his friend go to college? Did his friend graduate from high school? How much is his friend earning now legally? How much would he stand to earn in the future with a high school education or with a college degree?

Does what the educational system teaches go against his religion belief? Is it simply because American History is taught instead of Black History?

If that is the case, John should learn as much as he can about American History in order to pass. John can easily pickup an extra class on Black History in college or he can study it on his own. Sometimes you have to focus on the goal at hand and then fight the battle last.

One thing that always amuses me is the scholars and educators who criticize the educational system had enough sense to go through the process first. They were smart enough to play the game to get their diplomas, credentials, or degrees.

College isn't for everyone, but there are trade schools which can advance your career. As long as you have a plan, then you are working with something. You might have thoughts of opening up your own business. If you do the research and put the effort into it, then it can be done.

You will create a problem for yourself if your mindset is on doing nothing. So called pimping is nothing. A young Black man must learn to live for today but make some type of provision for the future. In most cases, pimping, selling drugs, robbing, stealing, or just doing nothing has no type of real current or future benefits.

Dropping out of high school shouldn't be an option not in less you are getting ready to strike the deal of a lifetime. When you choose not to finish high school, it really limits your ability to earn money legally for yourself as well as your family.

You must remember to never let someone else's opinion stop you from bettering yourself. You have to push forward whether it is getting a higher education or starting your own business. Another thing to remember is you have to do something in order for something positive to happen in your life. In other words that something might be getting your GED, enrolling in college, enrolling in a trade school, or starting your own business to advance yourself in this society.

Youthful Thinking

On Trusting Someone Else

So Trust Yea Not In A Friend

Friends might cause you to sin
Especially if they are pretend friends
Pretend friends like it when you do wrong
They will eat you out of a house and home
They love it when you are alone
Pretend friends talk about you on the cellphone
Because they are alone
They have a bright smile
Looking innocence like a child
But behind the smile is jealousy
Pretend friends really have a lot of envy
Because you are doing fine
They get a kick out of taking things from someone who is kind
Pretend friends don't like it
If you are making moves to become wealthy or rich
Because they don't have ****
Pretend friends don't like you to do right
They try to hurt you with all of their might
Pretend friends like it when you are poor

Pretend friends laugh to themselves when they think that they have more
Pretend friends like you when you don't have it
They like it
When you don't shine bright
Because they want the spotlight
So don't have confidence in a friend
Trust yea not in a friend
Pretend friends will not be with you to the end
Look out for those pretend friends
They will break your heart
Beware of the motives of their hearts
So trust yea not in a friend
Be cautious and wisely judge
It could be the person who you tell your secrets too
Who is secretly holding a grudge?
Against you

Enemy In The House

The sister fought her brother
They fought for no real reason at all
The brother fought his sister
They threw each other against the wall
They fought over a phone call
The sister told everybody about his dirty drawers
He said, "She was super tall"
Their hearts grew cold
Their secrets started to unfold
They talked about each other's private life
The words stabbed at each other like a knife
They were a close family
But their madness turned them into worst enemies

The son dishonored his father
The father dishonored the mother
The mother warred against her daughter

They couldn't get along
Because too many grown people
Where living in the same home
They had love
And most of their needs
Were met
But the mother and daughter never agreed
On an unusual night
They got into a fight
The daughter stabbed her mother with a knife
The knife nearly took her life
The daughter started to cry
She held her mother
Who was about to die
She apologized to her mother
Even though she loved her mother
Her father couldn't see
How his daughter was his wife's worst enemy
This is something that I found out
Your worst enemy might be living in your own house

The mother-in-law never liked her daughter-in-law
The mother-in-law lied about where the daughter-in-law was
She told her son
That his wife was with Tom
Tom was his best friend
His mother laughed as the relationship came to an end
His only brother revealed to him
What their mother had planned to do
The son realized that his mother
Wasn't telling the truth
He lost his faithful lady
Who had his baby?
Because his mother lied
The shock took him by surprise
His mother was filled with great jealousy
Turned out to be his worst enemy
As I have searched and found out
A man's worst enemy could be the man or woman in his own house

In Order For A Man To Understand

Don't put too much confidence in a friend
Who don't really understand?
The struggles or solutions to help fix the problems of the young Black man
Lean not to your own understanding
For man's understanding is nothing
But God understands all things
God understands planet earth
For God created it and all good things were birthed
From his imagination
The plants, animals, land, and man
With understanding from God
Foolish people become wise
People with earthly wisdom are unwise in His eyes
Because they don't fear God
Yet they search for a plan to help the young Black men
Never telling people that they must seek God with their whole heart

Wisdom Thoughts

You must ask yourself the question, are you a follower or a leader? A young Black man must know how to lead himself at times. In order to be an effective leader, you have to have some type of influence.

Normally, every friendship has the two aspects of leadership. It has an influencer or one who get influenced by someone else. If your friend or friends are the only ones who influence the group, you should make sure that they do it in a positive way. It is a healthy friendship if you can participate in the positive influences of the friendship.

If you are unable to influence yourself, you will always miss the warning signs when your friend is trying to misuse you, set you up, or if they aren't trustworthy. You will always be under the assumption that everything is fine.

Mother said it best, "watch who you hang around." Whoever you hang around can help elevate you or bring you down. That is why it is wise for a young Black man to hang around people who are trying to better themselves in life in most instances.

There are times when your presence can help motive your friends who never thought about doing anything in life. Your accomplishments might make them strive. There is no clear-cut rule, but caution is the key. You must use wisdom and avoid situations that you know aren't right.

I believe that there are some friendships that will last a lifetime. There are other friendships that are supposed to last a short time span like a week or two. The problem comes in when a young Black man doesn't know what type of friendship he has.

The money question is who are you hanging around right now? Is he or she really your friend? Because the people who you hang around has some influence on you whether you like to admit or not. Sometimes you can be unconsciously influenced.

I know that we like to say that "no one can influence me." The truth of the matter is we are getting influenced by life through our surrounding, by what we listen to, and what we watch as well as whom we associate with daily.

A young Black man must not dull down his senses when it comes to trusting in people. Most of the time, whoever have the most influence over you is the person that you trust the most. I am not saying, "You shouldn't trust anyone." I am saying, "You should trust the Creator and let Him help you filter out who you should trust and who not to trust."

Youthful Thinking

On Life, the Ghetto, and Other Things

Life Is Worth Living

People who are confused in their mind
Think about suicide
They call for help and
No one assist them with their problems
So they think about shooting themselves
They think it is the only way out
So they blame life before they flip out

He slit his wrist
Because he was lovesick
All those sad times
Flowed out his mind
He looked at the brick wall
It made him look small
Because the brick wall seemed very tall
He tried to climb it
But he fell back down it
Shaken up by his problems
His life hit the ground
He was looking for help

He cried within himself
Contemplating about life
Listening to the clashing sound
All alone with no one around
He had thoughts of suicide

He thought life wasn't
What it is cracked up to be
He thought the bullet
Would set him free
From the pain of reality
But life is like a rollercoaster ride
It goes up and down
So don't think about committing suicide
Learn how not to get upset because of your feelings
Because your life
Is worth living

It Is So Easy To Do Negative Things

It is so easy
To pull the trigger
It is so easy
To call people a nigger
It is so easy
To take an innocent life
It is so easy
To hate your enemy
It is so easy
To feel your heart with jealousy
It is so easy
To become a menace to society
It is so easy
To hate
It is so easy
To catch a murder case
It is so easy
To get into trouble
It is so easy
To be a racist

It is so easy
To be prejudice
It is so easy
To do injustice
It is so easy
To say I hate you

It is hard
To say I love you
It doesn't take any knowledge
Or a degree from college
To pronounce love
But a human being respect people
Any fool can shoot the gun
And start to run
But any real human being
With love in their hearts
Won't let these evil things
Overtake them with evilness
Because they will stay prayed up against all wickedness

For it is easy
To say terrible things
But at first it may seem hard
To let the pure love of God flow out of your mouth
like beautiful heavenly strings

Perished By His Lying Tongue

The man got hanged
By his deceitful tongue
He told lies for fun
Because he thought it will do no harm
He cried for mercy
As he hanged up in the tree
Wondering where he would be
If he wouldn't have lied to the Chief
The Chief gave the little man
Another chance
The wicked man
Lied again and again
The truth he never tried
He was happy telling lies
Everything that came out
Of his mouth
A lie here and there
He told lies everywhere
The man never told the truth

He was so used to telling lies
If he told the truth
Even he was surprised
He lied for all his days
This man's deceitful ways
Led him to his grave
The man was hanged
He perished by his lying tongue

Treasure Of Gold In The Sky

Speak loudly and clearly
So that everyone can hear thee
Sit up in the chair
Lift your head into the air
Look with a Godly stare
Stand boldly on your feet
So that everyone can see thee
Sing like a mockingbird
Pray so that your voice can be heard
Follow your dreams
For we are all kings
Don't let anyone tell you
What you can't do
Your destiny is up to you
When you fall
Stand tall
And you shall rise
Rise above the sky
You shall rise
If you only try

When you fall down
And start to cry
Don't get discouraged
Because you hit the hard ground
Rise up above the sky
For there is
A treasure of gold in the sky
And it can be found by the men who try

Stuck In The Ghetto

As the day dawn on a new light
Running for my life
Nowhere to go
Stuck in the ghetto
Staring out the window
Trapped inside my door
Trapped in the inside
Because there is too much violence outside
Trapped inside my door
Someone bar the door before
My heart aches with pain
Because the ghetto never changes
A young Black man's life has gone down the drain
Trying to make a fast stain (a robbery)
Another young Black man is out for fame
I guess in the hood money is the name of the game
My health I do maintain
As I looked out the window
The smooth breeze
Push against my nose

As I look through the screen door
As the world around me self-destruct
I look at a family that is really poor
I am poor too
But those children don't have a chance
Their mother steadily searches for a man
She has no plan for them to go to college
To enrich their knowledge
I thought to myself
What was the matter?
Dreams are shattered
Memories are gathered
As I look out my window and door
The cycle of life in the ghetto
So, I am fighting for my life
Looking for a dawn of a new life
But it seems that there is nowhere to go
For now, I am stuck in the ghetto

Wisdom Thoughts

A young Black man is faced with so much at times. There may be times when it seems like life itself is not enough. Life is more than enough if everything else fails. It is by God's grace that you are living. Once a young Black man understands the concept of living, then the ghetto, negativity, and his current environment really will not matter.

Once you embrace the fact that you are still living, you can begin to make a positive difference in your life. Living is baby steps. Baby steps with Jesus as your Lord and Savior is you leaping to grab a better future. I know someone out there might be thinking of suicide. I speak words of encouragement to you. Life can and will get better.

If you have fallen down, then Jesus will uplift you. He can help you rise up. Jesus can help you be a better father to your child and keep your tongue from lying. Only with his help, I am able to overcome as a young Black man daily.

Yet instill, there are some young Black men who think that they don't need any help at all. They think that they are capable of facing life's obstacles by themselves. In their minds, they do believe that all they need is self and no one else to make it in life. What is funny to me is that they even leave God out of the picture when he is the artist of us all.

There are other young Black men who believe in facing life's obstacles collectively as a group. Their motto will be something like *I Am My Brother Keeper, So My Brother Will Keep Me.* Those young Black men will make better progress because of unity. No matter how much progress they make as a group, they will surely fail if they leave God out of the equation.

The only way a young Black man can truly make it through life's obstacles is he must be plugged in to a power source. The most powerful power supply is in the hands of Jesus. This might sound like a cliché, but it is the truth. I can't put it any plainer than that.

Once a young Black man gets in hot pursuit of God, then he can begin to transform himself, his family, his community, his nation, and then the world.

Reflections on Today's Issues That Faces Black People

Justice Or Else

Justice or Else
Justice must begin with ourselves
We have to stop
Harming each other
For material wealth
Justice can only help
If it is impartial justice
Not justice suited to fit you
Because if I can manipulate justice to fit me
Then they can manipulate justice to fit them too
That type of justice
Isn't justice at all
It is almost as useless
As meaningless writings written on the wall
Justice must be justice in every aspect of justice
In order for justice to be able to stand tall
In order for the offended people to be able to trust in justice
It must be without a shadow of doubt justice for all

Black Lives Matter

It must matter to us
It must matter to me
Until it matters to us
It must matter to you
Or no one else will really care
It should be equally unsettling when Black people kill one another for senseless reasons
Not just when the polices do it for malice reasons
It should be labeled as treason
When injustice is committed by us
Especially when it is committed to us
No one death should be unjustified
But who is the judge and jury
In some of our eyes
Black lives matter
Some people pick and choose when it should matter
It should matter when someone commit a black-on-black act of violence
If we can't shout Black lives matter
Then maybe some of us need to keep silence

We should equally scream and shout Black lives matter

When someone else's sons, daughters, mothers, or fathers die of a senseless act of violence

Because Black lives do matter

In an instance, some life or lives have been shattered

All because in someone else's mind Black lives really didn't matter

Who Do You Protect?

Let's get it understood
Anytime there is a sworn brotherhood
There is a possibility that the truth will play the background
Most brotherhood outweigh the truth
But how can you put a muzzle on the truth?
How can you turn a blind eye to justice?
Yet it is done so easily
A percentage of the police only see the brotherhood fraternity
Which they were sworn into
It makes it easy to overlook common police brutality
Sometimes I have to ask myself
Mr. or Ms. Police which one is it?
Were you sworn in to protect your brothers and sisters in arms?
When will your moral senses know that it is time to sound the alarm?
Or were you sworn in to make sure that no harm
Will come to the public?

Or to rightfully protect us and them?

Even if you have to bravely stand up against the brotherhoods

To protect a regular citizen against injustice in all neighborhoods

The Code Of Silence

Some say, "The code of silence is dangerous"
Some say, "It promotes more violence"
The police say, "Speak out about the crimes that goes on in your neighborhood"
The people say, "Keep silent"
The people say, "The police should speak out about the crimes committed by the brotherhood"
The police's brotherhood says, "Keep silent"
Who wants to break the code of silence?
No one wants to break the code of silence when their group commits the act of violence
But both groups say, "Enough with the code of silence"
I am so confused
Both groups frown upon some violence
But there is a different meaning to the code of silence

Can't Think Straight

There are so many things
That plays in the mindset of a person
But a person who can't think for themselves
Their minds worsen
When someone fill their thoughts with untruth
They already don't know what to do
Now it is a bigger problem
Because they don't know who to listen too
Now they are following the wrong crowd
You will never know what to expect out of them
They are as unpredictable as a lion in the wild

Weigh Every Word For Truth

Weigh every word for truth
Sometimes people mix a lot of truth with a lie
Other times some people mix a lot of truth with a few lies
Then there are times when some people mix a lot of lies with a lot of truth
Some people just speak nothing but lies
It should come to you as no surprise
Some people speak nothing but truth
It might not be that appealing to you
Normally the perfect balance is great
This is one case in which balance isn't great
The only thing that is great is when the truth is only spoken in a clear-cut way
So that you can understand what that person is truly trying to say
I don't know what you prefer
But I will take the truth over a lie any day

The Women Movement

Why degrade your mother?
Why degrade your sister?
Just to uplift yourself
Just to pull the blame away from yourself
All women didn't participate in the Women Movement
Some women were at home trying
To get the men moving
But some of the men never started
They reversed roles and the women continued on moving
Some men continue on following
So who fault is it if you don't want to get a job
But you want to run the household like you are the head
News flash, when will it start
You must get up off the couch
I know the truth just hurt someone's feelings
I can hear someone saying Ouch!
I thought the head of the house
Supposed to be the one laying on the couch

Who Are You Following?

My brothers and sisters watch out for the trickery
Men are drawing followers unto themselves daily
You must know who is for the cause
Or who is lying to get your approval just because
Well, I have learned just because
You look black
You act black
But what does a Black person act like anyway?
I just had to ask
Is it because their skin tone is black?
Is it because of how they react?
What really determines if a person is Black?
To most people, your skin tone determines that fact
We must ask the questions about our leaders
Do their morals somewhat lack?
Does it really matter if they are not black?
But they fight for our issues that are under attack
The bottom line is who are you following?
Why do we march and protest?
We have some real unique catch phrases that we are hollering

But are we hollering for the wrong reason
Are our leaders committing treason?
So I must ask the question
You must ask the question
Who are we following?

Random Thoughts

With no particular person in mind
These are random thoughts upon my mind
We let the enemy confuse some of our Black men
Now what is the hell going on
Some Black men are blaming our Black women
For the Black men downfall
Watch out for the lies that are told
People with great titles like Dr. before their names
Are causing this newfound shame
Watch who you are following
Because they are throwing out the blame
Without a real solution
They are targeting the unlearned and unarmed person without the shield of God
They are straight shooting them up with useless mind pollution
What happen to uplifting each other?
Black is beautiful and a sister is a queen to her Black brothers
Now, it is popular to be a *****

Something is terribly wrong because they traded the Queen title to be a bad *** *****
And you figure
We hate it when a White person calls us a nigger
But some of us have accepted this term
It is almost like among some of us nigger is our first, middle, and last name
Some of us will stand in line to catch a deal
But won't vote
I am just keeping it real
But that is not all of us
Some of us just have to catch up
Maybe we should give up some of our role models
Who are not trying to help us come up?
But instead feeding us junk so we can stay on the bottom

Could There Be A Leader To Come Up Out Of Memphis?

Could there be a leader to come up out of Memphis?
A city known for the first 48
A city known for a high crime rate
A city known for hundreds upon hundreds of untested rape kits
A city where Elvis is the King
A city surrounded by conflict
A city that produced greats like B.B. King
A city that sometimes get overshadowed by racism
The Last city Dr. King
Spoke his final words
Where many people have something to say
But only a few are heard
Could there be a leader coming out of Memphis, TN?
I say most certainly
That leader starts with me
In every city, there are leaders ready to lead steadfastly

Wisdom Thoughts

A young Black man must not fall victimize to characterizing an individual by their race, their social status, or bad experiences with an individual or individuals. It is easy for the victim of such as things like injustice, racism, and racial profiling by the police to begin easily and unknowingly to react in a certain way. Our natural defense mechanism kicks in when we feel threatened.

It is a natural thing to want to fight for Black lives because we are legally known as Black (African Americans). It does seem like that it is a different standard when it comes to our lives, but we still have to carry the torch for all lives. As long as we know that all lives matter, we can consciously raise other people conscious mind on the fact that Black lives do matter.

In our pursuit for justice, we can't afford to take a compromise. There is no comprising with true justice. If justice is comprised, then it is considered injustice. A young Black man must know how to go about achieving true justice for all. We should know from experiences that if you fight fire with fire, the house will burn. A young Black man must learn how to use water in order to extinguish the fire of injustice.

In order for the young Black men to extinguish the fire of injustice, he must know what type of leaders that he is following. If his leaders are double talking and only communicating a little bit of truth, then his fire hose will only cause the flames to restart because he doesn't have enough water to extinguish the fire. Another way that a young Black man can extinguish the fire of injustice is by consciously doing the right things.

The right thing is accepting some of the responsibility and speaking positive things over your life in the middle of a treacherous storm. It is uplifting our sisters and mothers. It is for us to rightfully judge police officers on his or her own merits and not the entire group.

Thoughts About Family

He Is A Father To His Child

It is time for all men
To take a stand
And be a man
If you are doing wrong
Stop doing it
And take care of your home
Every old or young man
Should take care of his child
Whether or not you are a blue man or a purple man
So that your child won't grow up wild
All men of society need to spend more time with their family
Instead of running around in the street
So that our children will make a better society

If you make a baby
Take care of your child
Even if you are not with the lady
For that handsome son or beautiful daughter
Is your child

He or she is your seed
So you must provide for her or him

With life's basic needs
Give your child love
Show her or him how to keep her or his head above
The waters
Every man needs to stand up and be fathers
Whether you are a young man or an old man
You should take a stand
And be counted as a real man

For boys still play with their toys
But a real man
Will stand
He will stand up and carry his share of the weight
He is not afraid to admit his mistakes
He will do whatever it takes
That is positive to feed his child
And he will teach his child a respectable lifestyle
He will be there
When his child is sick

Showing his child that he does care

For only boys make babies
And leave it up to the lady
To take care of the baby
But on the other hand, only a real man
Will be able to stand
And face his responsibilities
Like a real man

He will provide for his family
They will never go hungry
He will do what he has to do that is positive
In order to feed his family
For boys still play with toys
A family's life, they don't enjoy
But a real man
Will always stand

He may never talk real loud
He doesn't brag about how many kids that he has
But he is a good father to his child

I Don't Have Time

I don't have time
To spend time with you
If I do
The lights will get cutoff
By the way, the rent is due
I would love to
But I don't have time
To spend time with you
I have a full plate
It is not up for debate
I have no time for you
I have to work
Now I am sitting here hurt
I have finally realized that
Not having time for your own family
Is one of my biggest mistakes?
Before I knew it
It was almost too late

If you don't have time for your family
You may wake up one morning
Asking your family, "today, what are we going to do?"
Their response might be, "We don't know
You didn't have time for us
We don't have time for you"

Father Where Are You?

Father where are you?
I can't sleep at night
Yesterday, I lost a fight
Father where are you?
No one to say, "Son is you alright"
No father with godly insight
Father where are you?

Father, you should have been the first man in my life
I was waiting on you
To tell me what is wrong and right
I was waiting on your guidance
I needed you to protect me
I am your daughter
Now, I don't know how a man is supposed to treat me
I long for your affection
Father and daughter time, I never knew
Father where are you?

Wisdom Thoughts

I heard some of my fellow young Black men say, "I had no other choices, but to sell drugs, rob, or steal. You don't understand the pressures of life. I have a duty to take care of my family, and this means by any means necessary to me."

I applaud any young Black man wanting to take care of his family. With the lack of positive young Black men today, society eagerly welcomes any man who wants to build up the family structure. The problems come in when someone wants to justify wrongdoing. They believe that wrongdoing is for a greater purpose.

The next time you are faced with a difficult choice. Ask yourself the following questions below.

Who will feed my family if I go to prison?

Who will feed my family if I die?

Those are the questions that you must ask yourself while you are trying to justify hustling in those streets. You must know that either way your family loses. They lose the most valuable thing in the process which is you being a part of their lives. There is always another way even if you can't currently see it.

I understand that desperate times lead to desperate measures. Please don't let those desperate times force you to choose bad choices. First THINK, what if I get caught tonight or die tonight is it worth it?

If you don't value your life, then what about your daughter? Who will give her away at her wedding? What about your son? Who will teach him how to be a man? You must realize that you are an especially important piece of the family structure.

Your family structure extends beyond the walls of your house. It extends to the community and to our society. Why? Every positive or negative decision affects us all in some type of way.

Once the family structure dwindles, then we are destroyed from within. There will be no one to instruct the children. There will be no one to discipline the children. Most importantly, there will be no one to teach them about God. If we have no fathers who teach in the family, then eventually ungodly people will instruct our children.

A young Black man must make the right choice. Our family is depending on us. Our children learn how to be leaders through our leadership abilities. In order for this to happen, we must be around in order for them to see a positive young Black man. Our example should be our family seeing us following God and fully trusting in Him.

Thoughts About GOD

So Many Questions

Who is this Jesus?
Are we black Israelites?
Are we the original Jews?
Are we the original Indians?
Are we African or American?
Is Christianity a White man's religion?
Does God really exist?
Those are the questions that we face
With everyone trying to prove their case
It is so easy for a young Black man to embrace
Anything that sounds pleasant to his ears
Anything that feels good
Anything that are forced upon him unconsciously by fear
With so many unanswered questions, then comes confusion
Ask God for yourself
Don't get caught up in the devil's many illusions

Wisdom Thoughts

   I am going to be honest with you. I see that there are many things that mislead us. For some of us, life has become a black and white issue. But to the true leaders, you must rise above that mindset. It is okay to be proud of who you are, but it isn't okay to make one race superior.

   It is not a black and white issue, even though the enemy plays us against one another. The real issues are evil vs. good, justice vs. injustice, wrong vs. right, or light vs. darkness.

   Where there is division among the people of God, there is racism, legalism, or ethnocentrism. How could one focus when so many issues are coming toward them so fast? We have to make split decisions based on what God want us to do. Some of our leaders have taken us off the path which leads to salvation when they try to uplift us as a people by spreading falsehood.

   I have seen so many people split the truth right in half. I have to ask myself whose side are they really on. If you refuse to ask questions, then you will be truly lost. You have to look at stuff a little deeper to see what angle they are playing. Is their angle to help you or is their angle to hurt you?

Let's be honest. Other races sometimes may experience feeling out of place in the wrong circumstances. Our experiences have led us to believe a certain way. One thing I do know is you can't beat hate with hate. One cycle within itself that has no paradigm shift can only lead to the cycle continuing.

I am not saying that there is no problem at all. We know that in our communities that the problems very much exist. I think some people would like to overlook it instead of fixing it.

How can you fix the problem of a young Black man? Some people have tried to fix themselves. Some people have asked the federal government to help fix it. Some people have united and still the problem still exists.

Our thought process must be fixed. Our minds must also be renewed. Once we begin to think right then we can begin to act right. We must block out the subliminal messages that is thrown at us daily. In search of the truth, we sometimes find a lie that was used as a substitute. This still isn't an excuse. We have to look to our Creator and pray, march, protest, and vote as a group not divided by race. It's time for something new and not what we are currently accustomed to.

Our grandmothers had a solution. Jesus was their solution. At times when my grandmother called on Jesus for help, her problems or concerns worked out every time in her favor. When her children got into trouble or the rent was due without a clue on how to pay it, she called on Jesus. Jesus seemed to always answer her in her time of need. Some of our modern grandmothers don't know who to pray to.

I thought my grandmother was crazy when she sung her songs. Many times my thoughts would echo Jesus will fix it but how long. Now, I have learned that he would fix it, but you must have patience. Over the years, my thought process has changed, and I now know that Jesus helps me to stand. I have grown to be an exceptional young Black man.

Today, I would like to introduce you to Jesus because most young Black men are without fathers or great role models. Jesus has been a great influence in my life. Jesus helped me release my anger which was a danger to me and society. Jesus helped me see things clearly. Jesus helped me achieve things that I thought I couldn't achieve. I dare you to believe. Jesus is the only one who can truly fix it.

At some point in your life, you have to make a life changing decision about God. So if you are still caught up in the black and white issue, then you might think Jesus is the trick of the White man. You might think that your grandmother was crazy because she was always praying. You might not believe in God at all. You might believe in something else. I challenge you to ask God for understanding of the truth, so that you can know the truth for yourself.

God is the only one who can give us wisdom to solve life's problems. God is sovereign, so he can solve all of the young Black men's problems and any problems that the world faces.

www.ingramcontent.com/pod-product-compliance
Lightning Source LLC
Chambersburg PA
CBHW070528100426
42743CB00010B/1992